RÍGSTHULA:
a new translation

D1784246

by Ben Waggoner

Troth Publications
2017

Published by The Troth
325 Chestnut Street, Suite 800
Philadelphia, Pennsylvania 19106
http://www.thetroth.org/

ISBN-13: 978-1-941136-15-7 (paperback)
978-1-941136-16-4 (e-book)

Cover image: Carved stone from Jurby, Isle of Man, illustrated by P. M. C. Kermode and W. A. Herdman, *Illustrated Notes on Manks Antiquities* (Liverpool, 1904)

Troth logo designed by Kveldulf Gundarsson, drawn by 13 Labs, Chicago, Illinois

Cover design: Ben Waggoner

Typeset in Garamond 18/14/12/11/10

INTRODUCTION

Though grouped with the mythological poems of the *Poetic Edda*, *Rígsþula* does not appear in the main manuscript of Eddic poems, the *Codex Regius*. It is written on the last page of the *Codex Wormianus*, a manuscript catalogued in the Arnamagnæan collection as AM 242 fol., and dated to the later half of the 14ᵗʰ century. The rest of the *Codex Wormianus* contains texts on Norse grammar and poetic diction. Because there is only one surviving manuscript of *Rígsþula*, it's not possible to cross-check different versions for accuracy. There are probable errors and gaps in the text as we have it. The end of the poem also seems to be missing, although the outline can be reconstructed from other sources, given in the Epilogue.

The poem's name sheds some light on why it was included in *Codex Wormianus*: the word *þula* specifically means a list of synonyms in verse. Although most of *Rígsþula* is narrative, the poem lists over eighty personal names, which also happen to be synonyms of the sort used in poetry. An accurate translation of the name *Rígsþula* would be "Rig's List". Skalds probably composed *þulur* as memory aids and teaching tools.[1] Several other Eddic poems are *þulur* or similar to *þulur*: the *Dvergatál*

("Catalogue of Dwarfs") included in *Völuspá*, the lists of names for natural features in *Alvíssmál*, and the lists of rivers and Odin-names in *Grímnismál*.

We do not know exactly when the poem was composed. It seems to contain echoes of very old myths that are recorded in earlier sources. Rígr walks along a shoreline when he finds the old, worn and inert couple Ái and Edda; in the *Völuspá*, three gods are walking along a shoreline when they find old, worn and inert driftwood that they shape into the first humans. There is also a parallel with Tacitus's account of the German tribes, in which a god named Mannus begot three major groups of people, the Ingvaeones, Istaevones, and Erminones. (In this case, however, the three groups of people are linguistic and cultural groupings, not social classes.)[2] Several scholars have pointed out that Rig's runic knowledge (as well as his sexual appetite) are not typical of Heimdall as he is depicted in other sources for the mythology, but are more typical of the god Odin.[3] However, other Eddic poems hint that Heimdall is the god meant here: *Völuspá* is addressed to *allar helgar kindir, / meiri ok minni mögu Heimdallar*, "all holy kindreds, greater and lesser sons of Heimdall". The section of *Hyndluljóð* known as *Völuspá in skamma* contains a reference to a god who is *sif sifjaðan sjötum görvöllum*, "related by kinship to the entirety of the hosts [of men]"; this god is not named, but he is said to be *aukinn jarðar megni*, "strengthened with the power of earth", and the same is said in a previous stanza of a god who is probably Heimdall. The skaldic poem *Húsdrapa*, composed just before the year 1000, calls Heimdallr *ráðgegninn*, "the one ready with advice," which seems to fit *Rígspula*'s characterization of Rig as one who knows how to speak helpful advice (*kunni ráð at segja*). All this suggests that basic concepts found in *Rígspula* date back at least a few centuries before the manuscript of *Rígspula* was written, and possibly back to heathen times.[4]

On the other hand, however old the Pre-Christian myths that it reflects, *Rígsthula* seems to show external influences from both Christian legend and Irish mythology. There are parallels with medieval legends about Noah's three sons. In the Bible (Genesis 9:11-27), Noah's son Ham accidentally sees his father dead drunk and naked, and Noah curses Ham's son Canaan and his descendants to perpetually serve the descendants of the other brothers, Shem and Ham. In an Old English version of the Biblical story, Ham is called the father of the servile race (*wælisc cynn*), Japheth is the father of free commoners (*oncyrlisc cynn*), and Shem is the father of nobles (*syðcund cynn*). A Middle English poem and a Middle High German poem reverse the roles, with Shem the father of free men and Japheth the father of nobles or knights; Ham remains the father of slaves.[5] As for Irish influence, the name of the god Rígr himself is derived from the Irish for "king", *rí* (genitive *ríg*). The custom of a householder allowing a guest to sleep with his wife is not otherwise attested in Norse texts, but it does appear in Irish texts such as "The Wooing of Emer", in which King Conchobor has the right to deflower the wives of any of the men of Ulster,[6] and in an Irish gloss that describes a king of the Hebrides who is allowed to sleep with any woman of his people, "one after another." Parallels also exist between Rígr/Heimdallr and the Irish deity Manannán mac Lír: both are associated with the sea—Rígr walks along the seashore, while Manannán rides his chariot on the ocean—and both father sons on other men's wives, with Rígr fathering Thrall, Karl and Jarl, and Manannán fathering Mongán.[7]

The idea of separate, physically distinct classes of humanity, born respectively to hard labor, farming, and rulership, is problematic for modern readers. *Rígsþula* has been called "a repellent poem" with "clear intimations of a kind of racism implicit in the description of the various social classes."[8] Certainly the idea that one group of people is born to do nothing but live squalidly and labor for others—and further, that that group is marked by physical features and coloring that those of higher station find laughable or disgusting—is morally troubling. Yet on closer examination, *Rígsþula* does not support the idea of fixed social classes in a divinely ordained hierarchy of superiority. The poem identifies the founders of the classes as three successive generations—Great-Grandfather and Great-Grandmother, Grandfather and Grandmother, and finally Father and Mother. The simplest explanation is that these represent three successive stages in the development of humanity, or at least of nobility—and furthermore, that all humans, whether kings or slaves, are of divine descent.

This is not enough for some commentators. Thomas Hill has stated that "The different orders of mankind are indeed fixed and unchangeable, but in the very beginning there was a certain kinship between the different orders of mankind. . ." He goes on to say that:

The most important point about the myth is that it denies explicitly the conception of common humanity. If a *jarl* and a *þræll* are both fully and to the same degree human, then the fact that the *jarl* lives in relative luxury while the *þræll* lives in want is morally problematical. But if they are in some fundamental way different from each other, then their difference in status is natural, like the difference between various species in the natural world. And this is the clear implication of the etiological myth of *Rígsþula.*[9]

But there are ways to interpret the poem that do not founder on Hill's dilemma. One could read the poem like this: Ríg fathers Thrall on the weak and nearly helpless Edda (great-grandmother). Thrall—who, despite his name, does not seem to have a master—labors hard, and despite his name, he and his descendants are able to better their station through the generations, until they give rise to Afi (grandfather) and Amma (grandmother), free and prosperous farmers. Ríg's son by Amma, Karl, continues to work hard as a proud and strong farmer, and his descendants continue to improve their station until their line produces Fadir and Modir, who have achieved noble status. The poem could be describing humanity slowly liberating itself through hard work, with Ríg progressively introducing more and more of the divine spark to those who have achieved success. While this "rags to riches" reading may seem a bit simplistic, it is certainly consistent with all the details of the poem.

There's some evidence that this reading is consistent with attitudes in the society that produced the myth.

Several Germanic societies were divided in a tripartite scheme similar to the situation in *Rígsþula*; the Saxons consisted of nobles (*nobiles* or *edhilingui*), free men (*ingenui* or *frilingi*) and servants (*serviles* or *lazzi*), whereas Saxo Grammaticus recognized the classes of nobles (*satrapa*), free men (*ingenuus*), and serfs (*servus*) among the Danes.[10] However, the boundaries between the classes of men in Norse society were not strictly determined by genealogy, and there was class mobility in both directions. There are plenty of saga episodes in which thralls are freed and become men of worth, or else their children become men of worth.[11] The association between swarthy skin and thralldom, and light skin and nobility, may seem obvious in *Rígsþula*, but it is deliberately subverted in other texts: Geirmundr and Hámundr heljarskin are heroes of noble birth, yet dark-skinned, while the thrall's son that they are swapped with is fair and blonde but of little worth.[12] This is not to say that being a thrall was especially enjoyable, nor that thralldom was morally acceptable by today's standards—simply that thralls were never considered a "separate species" of humanity. On the other side of the scale, more than one commoner's son in the sagas is able to attain noble status.

Musing on his role and responsibilities, King Ælfred wrote that

> *Hwæt, þu wast þæt nan mon ne mæg nænne cræft cyðan ne nænne anweald reccan ne stioran butan tolum and andweorce. Þæt bið ælces cræftes andweorc þæt nom þone cræft buton wyrcan ne mæg. Þæt bið þonne cyninges andweorc and his tol mid to ricsianne, þæt he hæbbe his lond fullmonad; he*

sceal habban gebedmen and fyrdmen and weorcmen. Hwæt, þu wast þætte butan þissan tolan nan cyning his cræft ne mæg cyðan.

You know of course that no-one can make known any skill, nor direct and guide any enterprise, without tools and resources; a man cannot work on any enterprise without resources. In the case of the king, the resources and tools with which to rule are that he have his land fully manned; he must have praying men, fighting men and working men. You know also that without these tools no king may make his ability known.[13]

The concept of the three orders is not present in the Latin text of Boethius that Ælfred was translating; Ælfred's mention is the oldest appearance of the idea in any Germanic literature, and quite possibly derives from an older way of thinking about society. Ælfred used the idea of the three orders of society to stress the unity of the kingdom. Ælfred did not consider the concept to be a hierarchy; all three classes were needed in the kingdom, or else the king could not rule.[14] We can read this poem, if we choose, not as a polemic in favor of eternally fixed social classes of slaves, commoners, and nobles—but as a description of a world in which even the poorest men and women bear a divine spark within; in which hard work and tests of one's mettle can enable the lowest-born families to rise; and in which the ruler is descended from all the social classes and unites them into one cohesive society.

I originally translated from the Norse text of Guðni Jónsson's *Eddukvæði*, but have since checked this against the diplomatic edition of the *Codex Wormianus* at the Project MENOTA Website, and also consulted the recent Íslenzk Fornrit edition. The parallel nature of the poem means that several lines and stanzas are repeated, such as the frequent refrain *Rígr kunni þeim ráð at segja*, "Rig knew how to tell them advice." At some points in the original manuscript, refrains that would be expected are missing, whether through scribal error or the need to save space on the page. Some translators restore these lines; I have not, but I have indicated the presumed missing lines in the footnotes. I haven't tried to reproduce the alliteration of the Norse poem, and I've held to a fairly literal rendering of the text, most of which is pretty straightforward. Still, I've tried to capture a rhythm and sound that will not be unpleasing when read aloud, as Norse poetry was intended to be.

I thank Dan Campbell, Erik Goodwyn, Seth Sample, and Wayne Morris for their help and encouragement, and Thomas DeMayo for contributing his translation of the extract from Arngrímur Jónsson's Latin rendering of the lost *Skjöldunga saga*. Errors in the finished product are entirely my own.

RÍGSTHULA

So people say in old sagas: One of the Æsir, the
one named Heimdall, went forth on his way along
a certain seashore. He came to a farmstead and
gave his name as Rig. This poem follows that story:

1. In old times, they said that Rig
went striding the green roads—a wise Ás,
powerful and ancient, mighty and vigorous.

2. He walked farther on the middle road.
He came to a house; the door was on posts.[15]
He went right in. A fire was on the floor;
a grey-haired couple sat there by the hearth:[16]
Ai, and Edda in an old headdress.[17]

3. Rig knew how to tell them advice.
He sat right down in the middle of the bench,
and the household couple sat on either side.

4. Then Edda took a lumpy loaf,
heavy and dense, packed full of bran.
She brought it there, in the middle of a plate.
Broth was in a bowl; she set it on the table.
Boiled veal was the finest of delicacies.[18]

5. Rig knew how to speak counsel to them.
He got up from there, got ready to go to sleep.
He lay down in the middle of the bed,
and the household couple lay on either side.

6. There he was for three nights all together.
Then he went on down the middle of the road;
nine more months passed by then.

7. Edda gave birth to a baby. They sprinkled him
   with water,
swaddled the swarthy[19] one with linen, named him
   Thrall.

8. He started to grow and to thrive well.
There was wrinkled skin on his hands,
his knuckles were twisted. . . .
his fingers thick, his face ugly,
his spine crooked, his heels long.

9. He began to try his strength further,
to bind bast, to pack up burdens;
he carried brushwood home all the dreary day.[20]

10. A wandering woman came to the farmyard.
Mud was on the soles of her feet, her arm was
　　sunburned,
her nose was hooked. She said her name was Thir.[21]

11. Furthermore, she sat down in the middle of
　　the bench;
the son of the house sat next to her.
Thrall and Thir talked and conversed,
they bedded down,[22] through busy days.

12. They bore children, lived together and were
　　content.
I think they were named Shriek and Cowherd,
Rude and Horsefly, Horny, Stinker,
Log, Fatty, Sluggish and Grizzled,
Stooped and Thicklegs. They put up fences,
spread dung on fields, took care of the pigs,
tended the goats, dug turf.

13. The daughters were Log and Clumsy,
Lumpy-Calves and Eagle-Beak,
Noisy and Concubine, Oak-Stake,
Tattered-Blouse and Crane-Legs.
The families of thralls are descended from there.

14. Then Rig went onward by straight roads.
He came to a hall; a door hung from the
   doorframe.[23]
He went right in. A fire was on the floor;
a married couple sat there, busy with work.

15. The man was shaping the top beam for a loom.
His beard was trimmed, his hair fell over his
   forehead,
his shirt fit closely.[24] A chest[25] was on the floor.

16. The woman sat and swayed her distaff,[26]
stretched out her arms, prepared her weaving.
A kerchief was on her head, a smock was on her
   chest,
a cloth was on her neck, brooches on her
   shoulders.[27]
Afi and Amma owned the house.[28]

17. Rig knew how to speak counsel to them. . . .[29]
He got up from the table, got ready to go to sleep.
He lay down in the middle of the bed,
and the household couple lay on either side.

18. There he was for three nights all together. . . .
nine more months passed by then.

19. Amma gave birth to a baby. They sprinkled him with water,
called him Karl. The woman swaddled in a linen cloth
the red and ruddy one; his eyes quivered.

20. He began to grow and to thrive well.
He began to tame oxen and forge coulters,
timber houses and build barns,
make carts and drive a plow forward.

21. They drove a woman home, with keys hanging down
and a goatskin outerdress; they betrothed her to Karl.
She was called Snoer and sat beneath a veil.[30]
They established a household, shared wealth,[31]
spread fine bedclothes and set up housekeeping.

22. They raised children, lived together and were content.
They were named Man and Comrade, Landholder, Freeman and Craftsman,
Broad-Shouldered, Yeoman, Bound-Beard,
Settler and Farmer, High-Beard, and Fellow.

23. They were called by still other names:
Wise, Bride, Vain, Haughty, Lady,
Spouse, Proud, and Wife; Shy, Forthright.[32]
The families of free men are descended from
   there.

24. Then Rig went from there by straight roads.
He came to a hall, the doorway faced south,
the door had swung open,[33] a ring was on the
   doorpost.

25. He went right in. The floor was strewn with
   straw[34];
the man and wife sat and looked into each other's
   eyes,
Fadir and Modir, playing with their fingers.

26. The man of the house sat and twisted
   bowstrings,
bent a bow and made arrow shafts.
But the lady of the house considered her arms,
smoothed linen, pleated her sleeves.[35]

27. Her headdress rode high,[36] a coin-brooch was
   on her chest,
she wore a long trailing gown and a tunic dyed
   blue.[37]
Her brow was brighter, her breast was lighter,
her neck was whiter than fresh, clean snow.

28. Rig knew how to speak counsel to them.
He sat right down in the middle of the pallet,
and the household couple sat on either side.

29. Then Modir took an embroidered cloth,
white from the linen, and covered the table.
She then took a light loaf,
white from the wheat, and covered the cloth.

30. She set out plates,
mounted in silver, on the table,
loaded with light-colored bacon and roasted fowl.
There was wine in a tankard, and gilded cups.
They drank and chatted—the day was ended.

31. Rig knew how to speak counsel to them.
He got up then, he made the bed.
There he was for three nights all together.
Then he went on down the middle of the road;
nine more months passed by then.

32. Modir gave birth to a boy; she swaddled him in
   silk.
They sprinkled him with water, let him be known
   as Jarl.
His hair was fair, his cheeks bright,
his eyes were fierce like a little snake's.[38]

33. Jarl grew up there in the house.
He started to brandish a shield, fit bowstrings,
bend the bow, make shafts for arrows,
fling spears, shake javelins,
ride horses, unleash hounds,
draw swords, prove himself at swimming.

34. There came out of the brush Rig walking,
Rig walking, and taught him runes.[39]
He gave him his own name, said that he was his
    son;[40]
he told him to take possession of ancestral fields,[41]
ancestral fields, old residences.

35. He rode on from there, through the dark wood
and icy mountains, until he came to a hall.
He began to shake a spear, he brandished his
    shield,
he made his stallion charge and drew his sword.
He began to stir up fighting, he began to redden
    the field,
he began to fell slain warriors—he fought for
    lands.

36. Then he alone ruled eighteen estates.
He began to divide his wealth, to offer to everyone
gifts and treasures, slender-ribbed steeds.
He scattered rings, and broke arm-rings apart.[42]

37. His messengers drove the wet roads.
They came to a hall where Hersir lived;
he had a slender-fingered daughter,
fair-skinned and wise; they called her Erna.[43]

38. They asked for her and drove her home,
betrothed her to Jarl; she walked beneath a linen
  veil.
They lived together and were happy,
increased their family and enjoyed their lives.

39. Boy was the oldest, but Child was second,
Baby and Heritage, Heir, Youth,
Descendant and Relative—they began to play—
Son and Lad—at swimming and boardgames.[44]
Yet another was named Kinsman. Kon was the
  youngest.[45]

40. Jarl's children grew up there.
They tamed stallions, bent shields,
planed arrow-shafts, brandished spears.

41. But young Kon knew runes,
lifetime-runes and lifespan-runes.
Furthermore, he knew how to help people,[46]
blunt edges, calm the sea.

42. He learned the chirping of birds, learned to
    calm fire,
to lull minds to sleep, soothe sorrows.
He had the strength and endurance of eight men.

43. He contended in runes with Jarl Rig;
he used tricks against him and knew them better.
Then he gained as his inheritance and was able to
    have
the right to be called Rig and know runes.

44. Kon the Young rode through thickets and
    woods,
he shot blunt arrows, he stunned birds.[47]

45. Then a crow said this—he sat on a lone
    branch—
"Why must you stun birds, Konr the Young?
Rather, your people might ride horses,
fell a host. . . .[48]

46. Dan and Danpr have more costly halls,
a more noble estate than your kin have.
They know well how to ride a keel,[49]
make their blades known, tear open wounds."

EPILOGUE

Rigus nomen fuit viro cuidam inter magnates sui temporis
non infimo. Is Danpri cuiusdam, domini in Danpsted,
filiam duxit uxorem, cui Dana nomen erat; qvi deinde
Regis titulo in sua illa provincia acqvisito, filium ex
uxore Dana, Dan sive Danum, haeredem reliqvit; cujus
Dani paternam ditionem jam adepti subditi omnes Dani
dicebantur. (In Dania igitur situm oportet Danpsted, et ut
ex historiarum circumstantiis colligere recte mihi videor, in
Jutia, som di Norshe kallede Reidgotaland).

Rigus was the name of a certain man, not least
among the magnates of his time. He took as
wife the daughter of a certain Danprus, lord in
Danpsted, whose name was Dana. Having thus
acquired from her the title of king in his province,
he left as heir his son, Dan or Danus, from his
wife Dana. All those subdued and won were now
called Danes after Danus' paternal authority.
(It is therefore fitting that Danpsted is sited in
Denmark, and, as I believe I have rightly inferred
from historical accounts, in Jutland, which the
Norwegians called Reidgotaland.)

Arngrímr Jónsson
Rerum Danicarum Fragmenta
(Latin rendering of the now-lost *Skjöldunga saga*)
English translation by Thomas deMayo

Móðir Dyggva var Drótt, dóttir Danps konungs, sonar Rígs, er fyrstr var konungr kallaðr á danska tungu; hans ættmenn höfðu ávalt síðan konungsnafn fyrir hit œzta tignarnafn. Dyggvi var fyrstr konungr kallaðr sinna ættmanna; en áðr váru þeir dróttnar kallaðir, en konur þeirra dróttningar, en drótt hirðsveitin. En Yngvi eða Ynguni var kallaðr hverr þeirra ættmanna alla ævi, en Ynglingar allir saman. Drótt dróttning var systir Dans konungs hins mikilláta, er Danmörk er við kend.

Dyggvi's mother was Drott, the daughter of King Danp, the son of Rig who was the first to be called king in the Norse language. Ever since, his kinsmen used the title of king as the highest-ranking title. Dyggvi was the first of his kinsmen to be called king; formerly, they were called *dróttnar*, and their wives *dróttningar*, and their retinue a *drótt*. But every one of their kinsmen was called Yngvi or Ynguni as long as he lived, and all together they were called Ynglings. Queen Drott was the sister of King Dan the Proud, after whom Denmark is named.

Snorri Sturluson
Ynglinga saga, ch. 17
(*Heimskringla*)

TEXT AND TRANSLATIONS

Bellows, Henry Adams. *The Poetic Edda*. Princeton, N. J.: Princeton University Press, 1936.

Bray, Olive. *The Elder or Poetic Edda. Part I.—The Mythological Poems*. London: Viking Club, 1908.

Bjarni Guðnason, (ed.) *Danakonunga sögur*. Íslenzk fornrit 35. Reykjavík: Hið íslenzka fornritafélag, 1982.

Chisholm, James. *The Eddas: Keys to the Mysteries of the North*. Illuminati Books, 2005.

Crawford, Jackson. *The Poetic Edda: Stories of the Norse Gods and Heroes*. Indianapolis: Hackett, 2015.

Dodds, Jeramy. *The Poetic Edda*. Toronto: Coach House, 2005.

Dronke, Ursula. *The Poetic Edda. Volume II: Mythological Poems*. Oxford: Oxford University Press, 1997.

Guðni Jónsson (ed.) *Eddukvæði: Sæmundar-Edda*. Reykjavík: Íslendingasagnaútgáfan, 1949.

Johansson, Karl G. (ed.) *Codex Wormianus*. Version 0.9.9; 1 April 2016. http://clarino.uib.no/menota/catalogue

Jónas Kristjánsson and Vésteinn Ólason, eds. *Eddukvæði*. Vol. 1. Íslenzk Fornrit. Reykjavík: Hið Íslenzka Fornritafélag, 2014.

Hollander, Lee M. *The Poetic Edda*. 2nd ed. Austin: University of Texas Press, 1962.

Larrington, Carolyne. *The Poetic Edda*. Oxford: Oxford University Press, 1996.

Orchard, Andy. *The Elder Edda: A Book of Viking Lore*. London: Penguin, 2011.

OTHER SOURCES

Amory, Frederic. "The Historical Worth of *Rígsþula*." *Alvíssmál* vol. 10 (2001), pp. 3-20.DO

Bugge, Sophus. *Norrœn Fornkvædi*. Christiana: P. T. Malling, 1867.

Byock, Jesse L. *Medieval Iceland: Society, Sagas, and Power*. Berkeley: University of California Press, 1988.

Carstens, Lydia. "Powerful Space: The Iron Age Hall and Its Development." *Viking Worlds: Things, Spaces, and Movement*. Marianne Hem Eriksen, Unn Pedersen, Bernt Rundberget, Irmelin Axelsen, and Heidi Lund Berg, eds. Oxford and Philadelphia: Oxbow Books, 2015. Pp. 12-27.

Chadwick, Nora Kershaw. "Literary Tradition in the Old Norse and Celtic World." *Saga-Book of the Viking Society*, vol. 14 (1953-57), pp. 164-199.

Davidson, H. R. Ellis. *Gods and Myths of Northern Europe*. London: Penguin, 1990.

Dumézil, Georges. "The *Rígspula* and Indo-European Social Structure." *Gods of the Ancient Northmen*, ed. Einar Haugen. Berkeley: University of California Press (1973), pp. 118-125.

Einar Ól. Sveinsson. "Celtic Elements in Icelandic Tradition." *Béaloideas* vol. 25 (1957), pp. 3-24.

Eriksen, Marianne Hem. "The Powerful Ring: Door Rings, Oath Rings and the Sacral Place." *Viking Worlds: Things, Spaces, and Movement*. Marianne Hem Eriksen, Unn Pedersen, Bernt Rundberget, Irmelin Axelsen, and Heidi Lund Berg, eds. Oxford and Philadelphia: Oxbow Books, 2015. Pp. 73-87.

Ewing, Thor. *Viking Clothing*. Stroud: The History Press, 2009.

Gisli Sigurðsson. *Gaelic Influence in Iceland*. 2nd ed. Reykjavík: University of Iceland Press, 2000.

Harris, Joseph. "Eddic Poetry." *Old Norse–Icelandic Literature: A Critical Guide*. Carol J. Clover and John Lindow, eds. Toronto: University of Toronto Press, 2005. pp. 68-156.

Hill, Thomas D. "*Rígspula*: Some Medieval Christian Analogues." *Speculum*, vol. 61 (1986), pp. 79-89.

Jochens, Jenny. *Women in Old Norse Society*. Ithaca, N.Y.: Cornell University Press, 1995.

McGrew, Julia H. *Sturlunga saga*. 2 vols. New York: Twayne, 1970-74.

Pálsson, Hermann, and Paul Edwards (ed. transl.) *The Book of Settlements: Landnamabók*. Winnipeg: University of Manitoba Press, 1972.

Powell, Timothy E. "The 'Three Orders' of Society in Anglo-Saxon England." *Anglo-Saxon England*, vol. 23 (1994), pp. 103-132.

Quinn, Judy. "From Orality to Literacy in Medieval Iceland." *Old Icelandic Literature and Society*, ed. Margaret Clunies Ross. Cambridge: Cambridge University Press (2000), pp. 30-60.

Roesdahl, Else and David M. Wilson. *From Viking to Crusader: The Scandinavians and Europe, 800-1200*. New York: Rizzoli, 1992.

Scher, Steven P. "*Rígspula* as Poetry." *MLN*, vol. 78 (1963), pp. 397-407.

Snorri Sturluson (Lee M. Hollander, trans.) *Heimskringla*. Austin: University of Texas Press, 1964.

— (Anthony Faulkes, ed.) *Edda: Skáldskaparmál. Vol. 1: Introduction, Text, and Notes*. London: Viking Society for Northern Research, 1998.

Tacitus (ed. Maurice Hutton). *Dialogus; Agricola; Germania*. Loeb Classical Library. Cambridge, Mass.: Harvard University Press, 1914.

Wechsler, Robert. *Performing Without a Stage: The Art of Literary Translation*. North Haven, Conn.: Catbird Press, 1998.

Wolf, Kirsten. "The Color Blue in Old Norse–Icelandic Literature." *Scripta Islandica*, vol. 57 (2006), pp. 55-78.

Young, Jean I. "Does *Rígsþula* Betray Irish Influence?" *Arkiv för Nordisk Filologi*, vol. 49 (1933), pp. 97-107.

ENDNOTES

1. Most manuscripts of Snorri's *Edda* contain a number of *þulur*; see e.g. *Skáldskaparmál* ch. 74, verses 412-516; ed. Faulkes, pp. 109-133.
2. Tacitus, *Germania* 2, transl. Hutton, pp. 264-267.
3. Scher, "*Rígsþula* as Poetry", pp. 398-399.
4. Amory, ("The Historical Worth of *Rígsþula*," p. 13.
5. Hill, "*Rígsþula*: Some Medieval Christian Analogues," pp. 82-86.
6. Young, "Does *Rígsþula* Betray Irish Influence?", p. 101; Meyer, "Wooing of Emer," p. 305-306.
7. Chadwick, pp. 185-188. In addition, see Gisli Sigurðsson, *Gaelic Influence in Iceland*, pp. 82-85.
8. Hill, p. 80.
9. Hill, pp. 80-81.
10. Dumézil, "The *Rígsþula* and Indo-European Social Structure", p. 120.
11. The best known is Melkorka in *Laxdæla saga*, whose son Óláfr pái becomes one of the wealthiest and most prominent men in Iceland, although this may arguably not count because Melkorka is the kidnapped daughter of an Irish king. But other examples include Ögmundr in *Ögmunds þáttr dytts*; Freysteinn in *Þorsteins saga uxafóts*; and several examples in *Landnamabók* (e.g. ch. 75, transl. Pálsson and Edwards, p. 40; chs. 98-103, pp. 52-53; and so on.) There is also the Norwegian landowner Erling Skjálgsson, who kept a revolving labor force of thirty thralls; his thralls could buy their freedom in a few years, and even receive his help in setting up their own enterprises. (Amory, pp. 6-7; see *Óláfs saga Helga* ch. 23, in *Heimskringla*, transl. Hollander, p. 261)
12. transl. McGrew, *Sturlunga saga*, vol. 2, pp. 15-24. See also *Landnamabók* ch. 112, pp. 56-57.
13. Quoted in Powell, "The 'Three Orders'", p. 103.

14. Powell, "The 'Three Orders'", pp. 103-105.

15. Translators differ on whether the doors of all three houses in this poem are open or closed. The literal meaning of *gætti* is "doorposts"; Bellows translates this literally without reference to whether the door was open or not. Most translators leave the door open, but Chisholm closes it and Hollander bolts it. Dronke (p. 216) argues that *gætti* refers to the space into which the door can be retracted, and thus that the door is wide open.

16. Most editions read *at arni*, "by the hearth", but Kristjánsson and Ólason read *af árni*, probably "[hair grey] from hard labor". (p. 449 n2)

17. *Ái* and *Edda* mean "great-grandfather" and "great-grandmother." The word *faldr*, cognate with English "fold", means a woman's linen headdress.

18. Sacrificed animal flesh was prepared by boiling and making broth; see *Hákonar saga góða* in *Heimskringla* (transl. Hollander, p. 107, 111). A possible interpretation might be that Ái and Edda have offered a religious sacrifice. However, boiling was the most common means of preparing meat for cooking, whether in ritual or not (Jochens, *Women in Old Norse Society*, pp. 130-131); there may not be religious overtones here. It's also been suggested that boiled veal is too rich a delicacy for Ái and Edda's table, and that these lines may have been moved from the missing description of Afi and Amma's meal.

19. *Svartr*, "swarthy", is the usual word for a dark complexion, and is often applied in the sagas to thralls, villains, and ugly people. It's not always clear whether it means dark skin, or simply dark hair and eyes; see Wolf, "The Color Blue", for a discussion. Really dark-skinned people, such as Africans, are called *blár*, not *svartr*—there's no "racial" division implied in the poem.

20. Amory ("The Historical Worth of *Rígsþula*," p. 7) points out the apparent contradiction that Thrall is laboring but does not have a master. If he's working for his aged parents,

carrying home firewood to keep them warm, his status would be that of a free man, albeit an impoverished one.

21. *Þír* means a female servant, as *þrall* means a male slave. Thir's clothes aren't described, but the fact that her feet and arms are visible shows that she's wearing less than the free or noble women described in this poem. Other texts confirm that slaves wore short clothes: for example, *Eiríks saga rauða* ch. 8 mentions slaves wearing nothing but cloaks that can be fastened between the legs. See also Ewing, *Viking Clothing*, pp. 42-45.

22. The line literally means "they made their bed", but the sense is probably "they went to bed together".

23. Literally, "the door was on a plank." Kristjánsson and Ólason suggest that Ái and Edda's door is open, Afi and Amma's door is half-open, and Fadir and Modir's door is closed. (p. 451 n14)

24. Bray assumed that "tight shirt" means a poor-quality or ill-fitting shirt. But the surviving evidence—both in artistic depictions, and in rare archaeological discoveries of the remains of actual clothing—suggests that Viking-era shirts were carefully pieced together and tailored to fit closely (Ewing, *Viking Clothing*, pp. 81-92). This line probably refers to a well-made shirt, not a poor one.

25. Lindow (*Norse Mythology*, p. 260) points out that since slaves could not own property, Afi's chest of belongings underscores his freedom. Dronke and Hollander, however, translate the word *skokkr* as "floor planking", not as a chest.

26. A distaff is a staff on which raw fibers are gathered at one end. To spin yarn, fibers are slowly pulled off the distaff and twisted by the rotation of a spindle.

27. Literally "dwarves on [her] shoulders." The brooches may have been called "dwarves" because they held up a woman's outerdress, like the dwarves in mythology who held up the sky.

28. *Afi* and *Amma* mean "grandfather" and "grandmother".

29. The lines describing what Amma serves for dinner are

missing. We may guess that the meal is somewhere between the coarse fare served by Edda and the delicacies served by Modir. Dronke conjectures that she served *iastarhleif, brattan ok brúnan, af byggmiölvi,* "a yeasty loaf, high-risen and brown, of barley meal"; she and Hollander also move the boiled veal from Edda's table to Amma's.

30. *Snör* means "daughter-in-law". Snoer, and also Erna, are specifically said to be driven in vehicles to their new homes, wearing linen veils. This resembles the ritual processions of veiled deity images in wagons, rites typical of the deities known as the Vanir (see Davidson, *Gods and Myths,* pp. 92-96 for an overview). Such processions may have been based on marriage customs, or vice versa.

31. The verb *deila* is often used for giving away treasure; *bauga deilir,* "ring-giver", is a kenning for a generous king or noble. Hollander is doubtful about this line, as giving away wealth is an activity associated with the nobility, not the free farmers. But *deila* could also mean "to possess", "to control", or "to share". It's also not clear whether Karl and Snoer are giving rings to each other (as Bellows, Crawford, Dodds, Larrington, and Orchard read it), or to other people. I've left my translation open.

32. Translators differ over how to render the daughters' names. I've followed Snorri Sturluson's own explanation of these names in his *Edda* (*Skáldskaparmál* 68, ed. Faulkes, pp. 107-108), where most of these names can be found.

33. Doors in Norse houses swung up and down, not sideways like modern house doors. The word *hnigin* literally means "sunk down", and Kristjánsson and Ólason interpret the word as "closed" (p. 451 n14) but the word is used to mean "open" elsewhere, as in the poem *Hervararkviða* in which the dead Angantýr says *Hnigin er helgrind, haugar opnask,* "the Hel-gate is open, the burial mounds are opening up." (Dronke, p. 223)

34. The Norse doesn't reveal what the floor was strewn with, but it was presumably straw—the words for "straw" and "to

strew" are related, in Norse as in English.

35. In the absence of ironing or laundry starch, pleats had to be sewn or pressed into clothing. There are fragments of women's pleated clothing from archaeological sites such as Birka. Linen smoothing boards and glass smoothers are documented from high-status female graves, mostly in Norway (e.g. Roesdahl and Wilson, *From Viking to Crusader*, #53-54, p. 242). In a society where all cloth is handmade, pleats are a sign of luxury, as they require extra cloth to make. Modir may be doing some sewing, but she's working on a fine piece of clothing for herself, rather than laboring over everyday cloth as Amma was doing. See Ewing, *Viking Clothing*, for technical details of Viking-era pleating.

36. Edda the mother of thralls was said to be wearing an old *fald* in stanza 3. Here we have a *fald* that rides high and is presumably more stylish and fine.

37. The tunic is said to be *blár*; there's been some debate over exactly what color *blár* was (Wolf, "The Color Blue"). Basically, *blár* could mean a range of dark colors from black to blue. According to Ewing (p. 167), *blár* clothing is dyed, while *svartr* clothing is made from naturally dark wool. The sense is one of luxury; in the sagas, owning *lítklædi*, "colored clothing", is a sign of wealth and power.

38. Fierce, blazing eyes are the sign of a mighty warrior, even as an infant. In *Bjarnar saga hitdælakappa* ch. 21, the hero acknowledges his son as *ægiligr í augum*, "terrible in his eyes". In the legendary *Ragnars saga loðbrókar*, ch. 9, the hero's newborn son Sigurd has *fránan brúnstein*, "flashing brow-stones."

39. *Rún* means both "letter of the old Germanic alphabet" and "mystery, secret knowledge". It isn't clear whether Rig is teaching Jarl the use of the letters, or secret wisdom, or both.

40. Literally, "said that he had a son".

41. The word *óðal*, translated as "ancestral", specifically meant land that had been passed from father to son for

several generations. The family that owned *óðal*-land could sell it, but retained the right to buy it back. One possible interpretation of this passage is that Rig must have once owned the land that Jarl must now reclaim by fighting for it. Another possibility, perhaps more likely, is that the land will become Jarl's *óðal*-land in the future, but only if he can win it and his descendants can hold it.

42. It was common for nobles to break up the arm-rings they wore and give out pieces. Such "hacksilver" is well-known in Viking-era hoards, and kennings like "breaker of rings" (*brjótr bauga*) were applied to generous lords in poetry.

43. A *hersir* is a local military leader of lower rank than a jarl. Erna's name may be related to *ern*, "brisk; vigorous"; Hollander suggests "the Efficient" as a translation, Bellows suggests "the Capable", while Dodds renders it as "Lithe" and Orchard as "Brisk". Crawford calls her "Eagle", derived from Norse *örn* (pl. *erni*).

44. Skill at boardgames is said to be a worthy accomplishment in both Norse sagas [e.g. Rognvaldr Kali's poem in *Orkneyinga saga*] and in Old English poems such as *The Gifts of Men*.

45. There is a famous pun here, repeated in several later stanzas, that I can find no way to translate. *Konr ungr*, "young Konr", sounds like *konungr*, "king". Compare this verse with the tale of King Halfdan the Old and his wife Alvig the Wise; they have nine sons who all become warriors and die in battle, and their names have become synonyms for "ruler" in Norse: Thengill, Ræsir, Gramr, Jöfurr, and so on. See Snorri Sturluson, *Skáldskaparmál* 64, ed. Faulkes, p. 101.

46. *mönnum bjarga* literally just means "to help people". However, *Sigrdrífumál* 9 uses *bjargrúnar* and *bjarga* in the context of helping women give birth. Chisholm, Dronke, Hollander, and Larrington all translate *mönnum bjarga* as "to help with childbirth"; Bellows, Bray, Crawford, Dodds, and Orchard translate it more generally as "to help people" or "to protect men".

47. Translators don't agree on how to render *kyrrði fugla*, literally

"he calmed birds." Kon either tames the birds (Chisholm), snares them (Hollander), charms them (Larrington), lures them (Bellows), slays them (Bray), shushes them (Dodds), silences them (Orchard), or kills them (Crawford). I've opted for "he stunned birds," because that seems to fit the fact that he's shooting blunt arrows (*kólfi*).

48. A half-line seems to be missing here. Dronke conjecturally inserts *hjörvi bregða*, "to draw a sword" or "to brandish a sword".

49. I.e., to sail a ship.

Printed in Great Britain
by Amazon